The Silkworm Goes to School

Written by Carol Adamo Johnson

Illustrated by Julie Bryant

Napa, California

This book belongs to:

_____

This book was given by:

_____

Illustrations and book design by Julie Bryant

sweetartdesign.com

Napa, California

2012

Dedication

This book is dedicated to my children,

Jolie, Greg, and Hollie.

And to my granddaughters,

Jessica, Jenna, and Rylee.

They encouraged me to turn my poems I wrote

for them, into books. And they continue

to inspire me every day.

Look for the silkworm
for fun and interesting
facts on every page!

Author Carol Adamo Johnson

A native Napan, Carol graduated from Napa High School in Napa, California and was selected to be the first "Senior Sweetheart". Now called "Homecoming Queen". A dance instructor, model, writer, and co-owner of the popular "Adamo Music Center", she has had many interests.

Carol worked for the Napa County Office of Education, in child care, with infants to school age children.

After she married and raised three children of her own, she decided to share her writing of short stories, poems, and songs and create children's books. She says, "Children give us purpose and make our lives complete."

Illustrator Julie Bryant

Julie lives in Napa, California where she was born and raised ... a Napkin!

The illustrations were created using digital watercolors and pencil on a digital drawing tablet.

To contact Julie Bryant go to *sweetartdesign.com* for her email, original books, samples of her book designs, and to view her sweet illustrations.

From China in a boat to a car,

something has arrived at school in a jar.

China ships raw silk from silkworms all over the world.

Our students have been given a pet.

A little silkworm they just met.

Today 60% of all silkworms are found in China.
The other 40% comes from India, Brazil and Italy.

Julia, Mary, Johnny and Michael,

you will be amazed at the silkworm's life cycle.

The silkworm's "life cycle" is the series of changes in his life.

In ten days he will hatch out of his egg and wiggle.

You can see him grow and you will giggle.

The tiny silkworm, right after he hatches out of his egg, is called a larva.

We give him the best of care,

by giving him plenty of air.

Silkworm eggs take ten days to hatch. They need fresh air and mulberry leaves to grow.

The lid's off the jar he is in.

The children look at him and grin.

Silkworms shed their skin four times in a row as they grow bigger and bigger.

Did you know you feed silkworms mulberry leaves?

In their cocoon raw silk they weave.

Ten billion pounds of mulberry tree leaves are eaten by silkworms every year.

Whether raised in a warehouse on a farm, or in a tree, his silk will make coats and scarves for you and me.

Some silkworms are raised on farms indoors in warehouses domestically, and some are raised in trees in their natural habitat.

The silkworm spins thread in his cocoon 1,000 to 3,000 feet for silk clothes to be made that are really neat.

Silkworms make 70 million pounds of raw silk after eating all those mulberry leaves.

As the silkworm grows, he sheds his suit of armor, then spins silk for ladies who dress up, with glamour.

When a silkworm sheds it's protective skin or armor, it is called molting.

To make a shirt or dress, takes 1000 cocoons.
The seamstress will make beautiful outfits soon.

Silk is one of the most exotic fabrics created by silkworms that they spin in their cocoons.

The boys and girls will have clothes colorful and bright.

Our silkworm will turn into a moth that's white.

Silkworms, in their cocoons, turn into a moth in about two weeks.

Extra Fun Facts:

* Silkworms were discovered over 5000 years ago in China.

* Silkworms produce silk that can be made into material, dresses, shirts, blankets, sheets and scarves.

* One of the first products in the world to get the "Made in China" tag was silk.

* The United States is the largest manufacturer of silk goods.

* The record holder for silk spun in a cocoon by a silkworm is 4000 feet long!

* The silkworm is from the butterfly family. The difference is the silkworm turns into a white moth and the caterpillar turns into a butterfly.

* A cocoon is a safe shelter for the silkworm.

* To remove silk out of the cocoon soak in warm water for 1/2 hour. When a single strand of thread is pulled loose, it is wound continuously onto a reel or piece of cardboard.

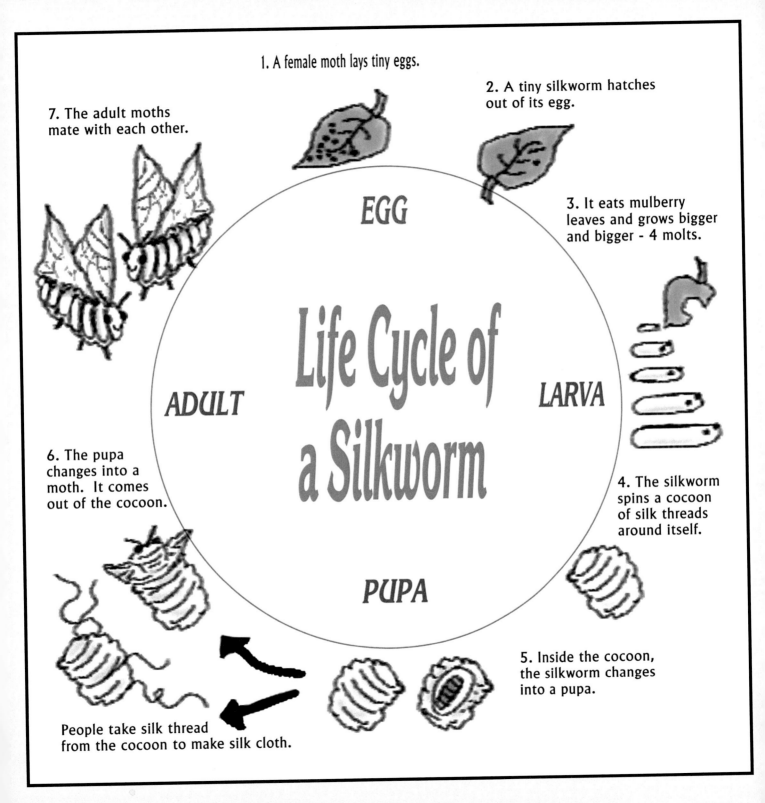

1. A female moth lays tiny eggs.

2. A tiny silkworm hatches out of its egg.

7. The adult moths mate with each other.

3. It eats mulberry leaves and grows bigger and bigger - 4 molts.

EGG

ADULT

Life Cycle of a Silkworm

LARVA

6. The pupa changes into a moth. It comes out of the cocoon.

4. The silkworm spins a cocoon of silk threads around itself.

PUPA

5. Inside the cocoon, the silkworm changes into a pupa.

People take silk thread from the cocoon to make silk cloth.

Notes on My Silkworm

_____

_____

_____

_____

_____

_____

_____

_____

Notes on My Silkworm

_____

_____

_____

_____

_____

_____

_____

_____

Made in the USA
San Bernardino, CA
20 May 2017